LEADERSHIP AND ENGAGEMENT FOR IMPROVEMENT IN THE NHS

Together we can

Report from The King's Fund
Leadership Review 2012

The Kings Fund>

© The King's Fund 2012

First published 2012 by The King's Fund

Charity registration number: 1126980

ISBN: 978 1 85717 640 7

A catalogue record for this publication is available from the British Library

Available from:
The King's Fund
11–13 Cavendish Square
London W1G 0AN
Tel: 020 7307 2591
Fax: 020 7307 2801
Email: publications@kingsfund.org.uk
www.kingsfund.org.uk/publications

Edited by Edwina Rowling

Typeset by Grasshopper Design Company

Printed in the UK by The King's Fund

Contents

Foreword

NHS managers have seemed like an endangered species in recent years. Politicians of all parties have called for cuts in management costs, and have outbid each other in the headlong rush to release resources to invest in patient care. The counter view – that a massive and complex organisation like the NHS requires top-class leadership and management – has not been well articulated.

It was for this reason that The King's Fund set up a commission to investigate the future of leadership and management in the NHS. Its report, subtitled *No More Heroes*, published in May 2011, brought together evidence from many sources to make the case for excellent leadership and management in the NHS. The report set out why managers are not only essential to the effective running of the NHS, but also have a critical part to play in supporting doctors, nurses and other clinicians to improve patient care.

The report argued that a new style of leadership was needed if the NHS was going to rise to the challenges it faces. Leadership must be shared and distributed, less reliant on heroic individuals and much more the property of teams and organisations. Effective leaders need to work through others to achieve their objectives, motivating and engaging followers and working across organisations and systems to deliver the transformational improvements on which the health care system of the future depends.

Leadership and Engagement for Improvement in the NHS builds on the arguments put forward by that commission and explores in more detail the role of leaders in engaging a range of significant others in improving health and health care. The debate on the Health and Social Care Bill and the government's far-reaching reforms to the NHS have reinforced the central importance of effective leadership and management at all levels, from the ward to the board and across traditional organisational boundaries. The purpose of effective leadership, put simply, is to improve population health and patient care; this needs to be recognised now more than ever.

The changes needed in the NHS to implement the reforms must happen at scale and pace. They will require leaders who cultivate a strong culture of engagement for patients and staff and who deploy a range of leadership styles and behaviours. The NHS Commissioning Board and Leadership Academy have a key role to play in developing existing and future leaders and embedding an engagement culture across the system. Equally important is the responsibility of every NHS organisation to value and support leadership and engagement in delivering its objectives.

As this report shows, there is strong evidence that leaders who engage staff, patients and others deliver better results on a range of measures. The business case for leadership and engagement for improvement is compelling at a time when the NHS needs to deliver unprecedented efficiency savings over many years.

We attach particular importance to leadership across systems of care to support greater integration of services around the needs of patients and populations. Leadership across systems is significantly under-developed in the NHS and must become a higher priority.

As last year, the report draws extensively on papers commissioned from leadership and policy experts focusing on different aspects of leadership and engagement. We are grateful to Beverley Alimo-Metcalfe, Pippa Bagnall, Richard Bohmer, John Clark, Angela Coulter, David Welbourn, Michael West and Jeremy Dawson for writing and revising these papers, which are available at: www.kingsfund.org.uk/ leadershipreview

We also invited a range of organisations and individuals to let us have their views on leadership and engagement, and have drawn on their contributions in preparing this report. In parallel, we arranged a lecture series led by recognised leaders from health care and the third sector, including those with international experience. The lectures were delivered by Richard Bohmer, Elisabeth Buggins, and Ciarán Devane, and they can be found at: www.kingsfund.org.uk/ leadershipreview

Several people contributed to the work that lies behind the report. I would particularly like to thank Kate Lobley for leading the work, Richard Vize, who prepared successive drafts of the report, and many other colleagues in The King's Fund and outside who have also contributed. I hope the result demonstrates the benefits of engaging many minds and hands in the work to be done.

Chris Ham
Chief Executive
The King's Fund

Findings and recommendations

- Recent research has highlighted that NHS leaders favour 'pace-setting' styles focused more on the delivery of targets than engaging patients and staff.

- Rising to the challenges that lie ahead requires a more nuanced style, with NHS leaders giving greater priority to patient and staff engagement; the involvement of doctors, nurses and other clinicians in leadership roles; and leadership across organisations and systems of care.

- The business case for leadership and engagement is compelling: organisations with engaged staff deliver better patient experience, fewer errors, lower infection and mortality rates, stronger financial management, higher staff morale and motivation and less absenteeism and stress.

- Patient engagement can deliver more appropriate care and improved outcomes.

- There is specific evidence that links medical engagement with organisational performance both from the NHS and other health care systems.

- The contribution of staff at an early stage of their careers to leadership and service improvement needs to be valued and recognised.

- The increasing recognition of the importance of integrated care, and the new structures put in place by the NHS reforms, require leaders to be effective across systems, including engagement outside the NHS.

- To support this, leadership development programmes should bring together leaders from different professions and different organisations within and outside health care.

- NHS boards should value patient and staff engagement and pay attention to staff health and wellbeing, for example by acting on the results of the NHS staff surveys.

- Every NHS organisation needs to support leadership and engagement in delivering its objectives, for example through effective appraisals, clear job design and a well-structured team environment.

- The role of team leaders in hospitals and the community is critical in creating a climate that enhances staff well-being and delivers high-quality patient care.

- The NHS Commissioning Board and the Leadership Academy have a key role to play in modelling and supporting the development of leadership and engagement.

Introduction

Engagement is not only a topic of academic interest; it has enormous practical significance. Put simply, organisations with more engaged clinicians and staff achieve better outcomes and experiences for the patients they serve.

Whether the NHS meets its three big challenges – driving up quality of care for patients and populations, finding billions of pounds of productivity gains, and making the government's reforms work – will depend on whether staff throughout the NHS see it as their responsibility to design and manage effective systems in their wards, clinics or practices, and feel empowered to do so.

Tackling any one of these challenges would be difficult; tackling all three simultaneously will be immensely tough, even with an energised and inspired workforce fully committed to the task. When many staff have deep concerns about the current NHS reforms and are worried about financial and service pressures and changes to their pensions, it is sometimes difficult to see a way through.

To stand a chance of making a success of all this, individuals and institutions need to rethink the way power and responsibility operate within teams and organisations and across the health and care system. The report of last year's Commission on Leadership – subtitled *No More Heroes* (The King's Fund 2011) – called on the NHS to recognise that the old 'heroic' leadership by individuals – typified by the 'turnaround chief executive' – needed to make way for a model where leadership was shared both 'from the board to the ward' and across the care system. It stressed that one of the biggest weaknesses in the NHS was its failure to engage clinicians, notably doctors, in management and leadership roles.

This second report demonstrates that engaging staff and patients is not an optional extra, but essential in making change and improvement happen. The evidence gathered during our review is clear: organisations with engaged staff deliver a better patient experience and have fewer errors and lower infection and mortality rates. Financial management is stronger, staff morale and motivation are higher and there is less absenteeism and stress. Patient engagement also brings benefits in delivering more appropriate care and improving outcomes.

This evidence makes a compelling business case for leadership for engagement and underpins the conclusions and recommendations of this review.

Making the case for engagement

Why engagement matters

For both patients and staff, engagement transforms the experience of the NHS. They feel respected, listened to and empowered, and are able to influence and improve care.

In their review of engagement for the government, MacLeod and Clarke (2009) quoted two companies performing strongly – O2 and Sainsbury's – who believed that recent growth was built on transforming their approach to their workforce using sophisticated engagement models. As Sainsbury's chief executive Justin King put it: 'In our business, with almost 150,000 people, engagement is a key concern... You don't even get started without engagement'.

If staff do not feel engaged they can spiral down into burnout, which can leave them cynical, exhausted and depressed. But where staff are engaged studies across a range of sectors show performance rises.

Evidence to this review from West and Dawson (2012) highlights a study by Prins and colleagues (2010) of more than 2,000 Dutch doctors, which found that those who were more engaged were significantly less likely to make mistakes. Similarly, a study of more than 8,000 hospital nurses by Laschinger and Leiter (2006) found higher engagement was linked to safer patient care. This benefit to patient safety alone is a powerful argument for health care organisations prioritising staff engagement.

So how do managers encourage staff to engage? West and Dawson (2012) suggest they need to give staff autonomy, enable them to use a wide range of skills, ensure jobs are satisfying – such as by seeing something through from beginning to end – and give staff support, recognition and encouragement. The personal qualities associated with engagement that managers should nurture include optimism, resilience and self-belief.

A study by Mauno and colleagues (2007) of Finnish health staff found that having control over how they did their jobs was the best predictor of engagement, even more than management quality. Similarly, Hakanen and colleagues' study (2005) found job control and manageable workload affected engagement. There were indications from this study that spending time with patients provided a level of engagement in its own right.

In a paper prepared for this review, Coulter (2012) makes the case for patient engagement. Shared decision-making with patients helps to deliver care appropriately; supporting patients to self-manage their long-term conditions contributes towards better outcomes; and care that is patient-centred makes a real difference to quality. Coulter also emphasises the close relationship between staff experience and patient experience, arguing that 'happy staff make happy patients'. The evidence and examples brought together by Coulter reinforce our core argument that leadership and engagement should be valued and supported.

What engagement means

The simplest definition of employee engagement spells out the relationship at its heart: it is when, according to MacLeod and Clarke (2009), 'the business values the employee and the employee values the business'. It recognises that every member of staff chooses whether to do the minimum, or do more.

The evidence to this review, and the literature on engagement, is littered with examples of staff who work harder, think more creatively and care more because they feel fully involved in the enterprise. The study by Salanova and colleagues (2005) suggests engagement improves performance in part because engaged staff are more likely to put energy into interactions with clients, while their positive approach may in turn motivate other staff, thereby creating a more engaged workplace. This may be one reason why engagement raises performance in health care.

Another possible mechanism is through engagement leading to improved operational control. Engaged staff are likely to exert more influence over the use of standard processes, teamwork and the degree to which there is a culture of improvement, all of which are factors influencing patient outcomes.

Engagement needs to be seen through the lens of the person who is being engaged. It is often described in psychological terms, for example, staff feeling energetic, determined, enthusiastic and even inspired. They are engrossed in their work and take pride in what they do. In 2007 the NHS National Workforce Projects team (NHS National Workforce Projects 2007) went further, describing how – similar to Salanova and colleagues' study – the enthusiasm of engaged staff was 'contagious'.

Within the NHS, engagement is often used to represent staff involvement in decision-making, or more generally the openness of communication with management. Indeed the NHS constitution itself pledges 'to engage staff in decisions that affect them and the services they provide... All staff will be empowered to put forward ways to deliver better and safer services for patients and their families'.

Patient experience is strongly correlated with staff engagement but engaging patients is important in its own right. By patient engagement we mean the degree to which people are empowered to be fully involved in their care, share in decision-making, and work with clinicians to meet their needs. While the practicalities of patient engagement differ from that of staff, this review provides strong evidence that both staff and patient engagement are grounded in values of openness, collaboration, seeing the world through the eyes of others, and listening to and supporting each individual.

Staff engagement in the NHS

Work undertaken for this review by West and Dawson (2012) summarised evidence on staff engagement in the NHS and the relationship with organisational performance.

There has been an annual staff survey in the English NHS since 2003, and questions on engagement were introduced in 2009. It is measured using three dimensions: psychological engagement (similar to motivation), advocacy and involvement.

Psychological engagement is judged by three questions: 'I look forward to going to work', 'I am enthusiastic about my job', and 'time passes quickly'.

Advocacy is measured by whether an employee would recommend their organisation as a place to work and be treated.

Involvement is gauged by three questions: 'I am able to make suggestions to improve the work of my team', 'there are frequent opportunities for me to show initiative', and 'I am able to make improvements happen'.

Analysis of the 2011 survey (Department of Health 2011b) by West and Dawson for this review shows significant differences between types of trust, and staff groups, in engagement. While acute, primary care and mental health trusts had broadly comparable engagement levels, ambulance trusts generally had much lower scores. The 2005 government report on the ambulance service, *Taking Healthcare to the Patient* (Department of Health 2005), highlighted low investment in staff development and a tendency to appoint managers on the basis of clinical or operational expertise rather than aptitude for leadership. It called for the service to be 'led in a way that promotes collaboration, builds networks and encourages management and staff development'.

Staff who say they have an interesting job report higher levels of engagement, as do those with good support from their manager. Other factors include feeling the job makes a difference, being clear on the objective and being involved in decisions. Engaged staff were less likely to suffer from stress.

Evidence from West and colleagues (2002, 2006) demonstrates a strong link between appraisal and engagement. The staff survey asks if staff had an appraisal in the past year, whether it helped them do their job, whether clear objectives were set, and whether the employee left the appraisal feeling valued. If the answers to all these questions were 'yes', then the appraisal was judged to have been well structured. In 2011, 80 per cent of respondents had an appraisal, but only 35 per cent had a well-structured one. While those employees who had a well-structured appraisal had far higher engagement than those who did not, poorly structured appraisals left staff feeling worse than if they had not had one.

How staff engagement raises health care performance

West and Dawson (2012) compared engagement scores in the NHS staff survey with a wide range of outcome data. They showed that patient experience improves, inspection scores are higher and infection and mortality rates are lower where there is strong staff engagement.

Patient experience is closely correlated with the 'advocacy' element of engagement – recommending the organisation as a place to work and be treated. This could be because staff who see satisfied patients are more likely to believe the care is good. Trusts with lower infection rates have more staff who feel they can contribute towards improvements.

Engagement is critical in explaining absenteeism. The effects are such that high engagement was associated with much lower absenteeism than low or moderate levels of engagement. Staff engagement is also correlated with turnover, with high levels of engagement associated with lower levels of turnover.

The relationship between staff engagement and staff absenteeism, and staff engagement and trust performance as measured by the Annual Health Check (AHC), is illustrated in Figures 1 and 2, overleaf.

Patient engagement in the NHS

Engaging patients in their care has been an increasingly important focus of health policy. In 2000 the NHS Plan (Department of Health 2000) talked of shaping services around the needs and preferences of individual patients. Seven years later 'world class commissioning' attempted to embed patient and public involvement in how services were commissioned.

In 2008 the Next Stage Review (Department of Health 2008) said the NHS must 'empower patients with greater choice, better information and more control and influence', and put patient experience alongside safety and effectiveness as one of

Figure 1 Absenteeism by levels of engagement

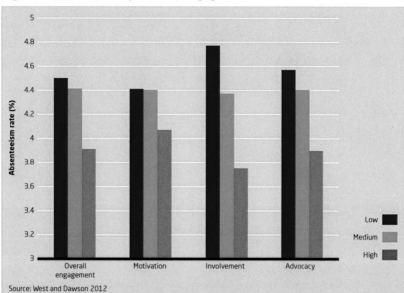

Source: West and Dawson 2012

Figure 2 Overall engagement by AHC performance

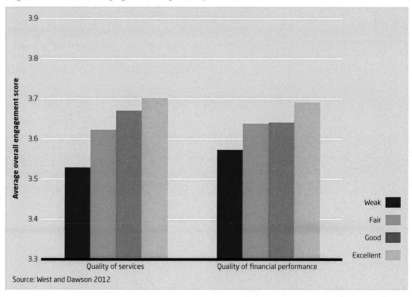

Source: West and Dawson 2012

the three measures of service quality. In 2009 the NHS constitution (Department of Health 2009b) stressed the right of patients to influence their own care and local services.

In 2010 the coalition government's health White Paper *Equity and Excellence: Liberating the NHS* (Department of Health 2010) stressed that the goal of world-class health care 'can only be realised by involving patients fully in their own care, with decisions made in partnership with clinicians, rather than by clinicians alone'. It called for shared decision-making to become the norm.

There are beacons of good practice in mental health, such as South Essex Partnership University NHS Foundation Trust, which sees its service users as experts in the trust's performance and engages them in a variety of imaginative ways, including mystery shopping. As we discuss below, there are also some acute trusts that have found innovative ways of engaging with patients and using evidence on patient experience to improve the quality of care.

Notwithstanding these examples, much remains to be done to strengthen patient engagement in the different ways Angela Coulter (2012) describes in her paper for this review.

The role of leadership in engagement

The dominance of 'pace-setter' leadership in the NHS

The Hay Group consultancy identifies six main leadership styles (Santry 2011). The dominant NHS approach is known as 'pace-setter' – typified by laying down demanding targets, leading from the front, often being reluctant to delegate, and collaborating little – and is the consequence of the health service focusing on process targets, with recognition and reward dependent on meeting them.

Targets have secured impressive improvements in access, such as shorter waiting lists and faster treatment in emergency departments. However, they have done so at the cost of too many NHS leaders using the pace-setter approach to the exclusion of other leadership styles, such as 'affiliative' – creating trust and harmony – or 'coaching'. Truly high-performing leaders deploy a range of leadership approaches depending on the demands of each situation.

There is growing evidence that the NHS needs to break with the command and control, target-driven approach. The Commission on Dignity in Care for Older People (2012) identified the top-down culture as a prime cause of poor care, concluding: 'If senior managers impose a command and control culture that demoralises staff and robs them of the authority to make decisions, poor care will follow'.

In a similar vein, counsel to the inquiry led by Robert Francis QC into the failings at Mid Staffordshire NHS Foundation Trust said the failure in clinical governance at the trust was caused by 'a lack of clinical engagement... Whatever then gets turned out by the Department of Health, whatever initiatives are started at the top, unless the clinical soil is fertile, the seeds will inevitably fall to stony ground at trust level' (Mid Staffordshire NHS Foundation Trust Inquiry 2011).

Pace-setting leadership reflects the focus on improving the performance of the NHS from a low base over the last decade or more. It needs to be complemented by other styles of leadership in the next stage of reform. This was recognised in Lord Darzi's 2008 review (Department of Health 2008), which particularly emphasised the need to engage doctors and other clinicians in leading change and service improvement for patients. It is even more important in the current climate, not least to support NHS leaders to engage with partner organisations in making improvements across local systems of care, for example through closer integration of services.

A different approach to leadership

In 2008 the Chartered Institute of Personnel and Development built a model of post-heroic leadership which stresses that leadership is not about being an extraordinary person, but being open, accessible and transparent. It emphasises teamwork, collaboration and 'connectedness', and removing barriers to communication and original thinking. It reflects a desire to see the world through the eyes of others, to take on board their concerns and perspectives and to work with their ideas (Alimo-Metcalfe and Alban-Metcalfe 2008).

The model posits an environment in which the status quo is challenged, ideas are listened to and valued and innovation and entrepreneurialism are encouraged. A culture that supports development is created in which the leader is a role model for learning, and in which inevitable mistakes are exploited for their learning opportunities.

So leadership acts as a 'cognitive catalyst'. Gone is the heroic individual with a monopoly on the vision; it is replaced by a commitment to building shared visions with a range of stakeholders. It exploits the diversity of perspectives and the wealth of experiences, strengths and potential in the organisation. It's teamwork.

For the leader this approach is more challenging because of the skill and risk involved, and more exciting because of the possibilities engagement will bring. It is also far more achievable; being seen as the source of all wisdom will often end in failure.

Implications for the NHS

The culture of the NHS as the government's reforms are implemented will be heavily influenced by the NHS Commissioning Board, alongside the Care Quality Commission and Monitor. The Board needs to break from the command and control approach of the past and demonstrate convincingly that distributed leadership and engagement are now core values for the service.

The Department of Health has stated in its publication *Developing the NHS Commissioning Board* (Department of Health 2011a) that it will seek to support and hold to account clinical commissioning groups, not domineer or micro-manage them. Importantly there is recognition that this requires the Board to be more effective at coaching to enable everyone at each level in the system to give their best. The Board is committed to embedding a new change model which will work from the position of generating shared purpose, goals and values at all levels.

Developing the NHS Commissioning Board sets out the intention that the Board will work in partnership across boundaries and develop mutually supportive relationships. This will require development of its collaborative capabilities. Engagement and involvement are identified as core skills for staff in the new organisation. It follows that successful system leadership will require a wider range of leadership styles than has often been deployed in the NHS in the past.

The success of the Board in delivering this shift will be crucial to allow a diversity of leadership styles to flourish. This flourishing needs to happen above all in the new clinical commissioning groups. GPs and managers leading commissioning will have to build alliances, share values, listen, empathise and negotiate to secure better services for patients. Engagement needs to be the hallmark of their leadership, while the NHS Commissioning Board needs to give commissioning groups the space and support to engage with their local partners.

The NHS Leadership Academy, in its role of setting national standards for leadership, should vigorously promote the importance of a diversity of leadership styles and the centrality of patient and staff engagement in leading quality improvement. To help the service move away from over-reliance on the pace-setter approach, the Academy will need to develop the skills of a generation of managers who have secured promotion and success in the target-driven culture.

This has started to happen in the Top Leaders Programme (NHS Leadership Academy 2012) and now needs to be taken forward with urgency. One practical way in which this could be done is by supporting leadership development that brings together leaders from different organisations and backgrounds with a focus on leading improvement across systems of care. As we discuss below, leading across systems of care is a critical issue for the future and one that has been relatively neglected in the recent past.

Implications for leadership development

The practicalities of improving health care provide further evidence of the superiority of distributed leadership over heroic leadership, because it requires activity right across the system, from ward and hospital department to the GP, community services and social care, involving the whole spectrum of care professionals. In exceptional organisations, such as Intermountain Healthcare in the United States or Jönköping County Council in Sweden, leadership for improvement involves reforming the system through a sustained effort, often over many years (Baker 2011). This effort is designed to create the ways of working, people development, culture, systems and environment that are the conditions for promoting improvement.

In a submission to this review, the Advancing Quality Alliance argued that successful leadership of health care improvement combines three sets of skills: service-specific knowledge, improvement know-how and change management skills.

The need for service-specific knowledge – understanding how clinical services work and what is required to provide high-quality care – means clinicians need to be among the people leading the change. For clinicians embedded in the service, the challenge is to use their knowledge without being wedded to the status quo.

Mastering quality improvement know-how – increasingly being described as the science of health care improvement – includes techniques adapted from production engineering such as 'lean', together with methods such as clinical audit and research.

The third skill – change management – includes handling relationships, building coalitions of support, countering resistance to change and communicating a vision to staff, patients, the public and wider stakeholders. Engagement of staff and patients is central to this aspect of health care improvement.

To make these points is to underline the importance not just of a new style of leadership but also of leadership development. Increasingly the NHS needs managerial and clinical leaders who have learned the skills of improvement and are able to put them into practice. This is the clear lesson from both Intermountain Healthcare and Jönköping County Council where there is strong evidence of the link between high levels of staff engagement and development and organisational performance (Baker 2011).

Organisations such as these not only invest in formal leadership development, but also provide venues for developing leaders to hone their skills backed up by systems that support their leadership work. At Intermountain Healthcare, for example, there are many opportunities for clinicians to become involved in day-to-day management and in long-term improvement work. As Richard Bohmer showed in a paper for this review, the managerial and economic language associated with health care leadership – often a turn-off for clinicians – is replaced with a much more comfortable clinical language; an 'evidence-based reduction of overuse and underuse' instead of 'cost control' (Bohmer 2012).

Engaging different groups

Engagement in health care involves one group that is far more powerful than it thinks – doctors – and another that is far less powerful than it should be – patients. Engagement with both is central to improving patient care. In this section we will also examine nurse and allied health professional leadership, the trust board's role in setting organisational culture, and how leaders can engage with the rest of the health system to improve care.

Engagement of staff and patients is underpinned by a common set of values. In the context of the Chartered Institute of Personnel and Development leadership model (Alimo-Metcalfe and Alban-Metcalfe 2008) it can be seen that organisations which engage both groups will be open and accessible, will emphasise collaboration, will remove barriers to communication, see the world through the eyes of others, take on board their concerns and perspectives and work with their ideas. Each individual will be valued, supported and listened to; the patient engagement mantra of 'no decision about me without me' applies just as well to staff.

Engaging staff

Organisations developing leadership programmes to engage staff need to do so in ways that bring different groups together. In evidence to this review the Royal College of Surgeons argued that for too long leadership initiatives targeted at separate groups – doctors, managers and so on – have reinforced differences and done nothing to encourage collaboration. The college believes leadership development that brings staff together will improve care.

Engagement is fostered through staff having jobs with meaningful, clear tasks, some autonomy to manage their work, involvement in decision-making and supportive line managers. They are part of a well-structured team in an organisation that is focused on quality and celebrates success. In short, engaged staff feel valued, respected and supported.

But engagement means far more than having an engagement strategy. Mechanistic approaches that lack sincerity will soon be found out because engagement is built on authenticity. Organisations that engage both staff and patients have strong values of trust, fairness and respect which are consistently articulated and acted upon.

One example is the use of the Schwartz Round®. This is a supportive approach, originally developed in the United States, in which staff from all disciplines come together once a month to reflect on the non-clinical aspects of their work, discussing difficult emotional and social issues arising out of patient care day-to-day. Pilots run in partnership with The King's Fund at Royal Free Hampstead NHS Trust and Gloucestershire Hospitals NHS Foundation Trust indicated that the success of the Rounds in the United States could be replicated here, and other organisations are now starting the programme (Goodrich and Levenson 2012).

From crisis to foundation status

In 2006 Blackpool, Fylde and Wyre Hospital Trust was in crisis with a projected deficit of £21 million. It wanted to secure foundation trust status but had too many sites, major bed pressures, a lack of clinical engagement and high costs.

Working with trade unions the trust undertook an extensive public consultation to agree a way forward, and decided to deliver the changes needed in one year. These included closing outlying sites, centralising day surgery, relocating services such as stroke care and cutting 200 beds and more than 500 posts.

Engagement with staff emphasised clinical improvement. Plans were agreed with the Clinical Policy Forum, the Patients' Forum and the staff side. The trust achieved foundation trust status and delivered its workforce plan, and is convinced that staff engagement was crucial. The emphasis now is on continuous improvement and staff development. Engagement is monitored through staff surveys and there is a well-developed staff awards system.

The foundation trust is particularly proud of its Partnership for Learning project, backed by Unison, to improve literacy and numeracy, raise motivation and confidence and widen involvement in learning. More than 1,000 staff have participated.

Engaging with staff and patients using Listening into Action (LiA)

Sandwell and West Birmingham NHS Trust introduced the Listening into Action (LiA) approach to staff engagement in 2008, after poor staff survey results. LiA identifies what needs to change to improve the service to patients and the lives of staff. It involves asking people three questions – what is positive about their experience, what is less positive and what should change.

It began with five 'big conversations' with large staff groups. They wanted improvements in communication, equipment, customer care and the environment. Changes such as better lighting were made quickly to demonstrate staff engagement was making a difference. More than 100 teams have now participated, and LiA is being used with patients and relatives in services including stroke care, maternity, critical care and audiology.

There have been many improvements for patients including:

- better contrasting colours in the ophthalmology unit
- better food for women after giving birth
- the introduction of patient diaries on critical care
- access to 24-hour CT scanning.

Improvements for staff include better food in the canteen, better equipment management and more communication with the chief executive. LiA has contributed to sharp improvements in scores in the national staff survey. Some of the most powerful changes have been in the way staff treat each other – clinic rooms are left tidier and people take more responsibility for things such as replacing stock.

Engaging patients

Engagement with patients means turning the promises in the NHS constitution about involving people in decisions about their care into reality. At a structural level patients are engaged through a variety of mechanisms, such as patient forums, advocates, foundation trust governors, involvement in co-designing services and, as part of the reforms, clinical commissioning groups, HealthWatch England, local HealthWatch organisations and health and well-being boards.

All these can be important in giving patients a voice, but personal engagement with individual patients is what matters most. This not only shapes care for that person but enables clinicians and managers to see services through patients' eyes, helping to mould culture and practice to secure more responsive and sensitive care. When done well, patient engagement also enables patients to be more in control of their health and well-being, sharing in decision-making with clinicians through access to information and advice about the risks and benefits of treatment options.

Most people want to play an active part in their own care and expect health professionals to help them do so. This is not just a middle-class concern; studies have shown that people from low literacy groups can benefit more than most when efforts are made to inform and empower them (eg, Volandes *et al* 2011). But many clinicians are reluctant to involve patients.

In a paper for this review Angela Coulter argues that greater patient engagement is the best way to ensure the NHS is sustainable because it helps deliver the right care, strengthens patients' ability to manage long-term conditions and improves outcomes (Coulter 2012). She describes a range of projects aiming to find out what patients and the public want, but which collectively hardly scratch the surface of the organisational and cultural change required if the NHS is to become patient-centred. Barriers to changing entrenched clinical styles include lack of awareness, incentives and training, time pressures, a desire to keep a distance from patients' emotional problems and fear of losing power.

There is also an unwillingness to experiment with new ways of relating to patients, a consequence of a risk-averse culture that discourages innovation. Some NHS organisations are now developing a strategic approach to patient engagement. For example, since 2009 Northumbria Healthcare NHS Foundation Trust has had a director of patient experience leading an ambitious change programme with strong support from the board.

Their goal is to understand what matters most to patients and staff and to use that to guide the trust's work. Regular face-to-face patient surveys are central to the new approach. Fortnightly surveys are carried out with about 400 patients at a time. Results are presented to departments, wards and consultants, reviewed by the board and published on the trust's intranet, with highlights displayed in public areas.

The results include patient survey scores for named consultants. Some doctors resisted this approach, but it is now widely accepted and referred to during appraisals. Variations help identify both excellent performance and areas that need improvement. Rapid feedback enables staff to see the result of any improvements they have made, providing encouragement and reward.

The programme has led to small and big changes including inexpensive improvements to ward facilities and the introduction of stroke support volunteers to help patients and carers. Six-monthly snapshots have shown consistent and significant improvements in care quality across the trust.

The role of leadership in patient engagement

The changes at Northumbria were initiated by clinical and managerial leaders committed to learning from patients' experiences. They focused on clear goals, were ambitious, strategic and willing to take risks such as challenging their colleagues to change. Staff were helped to view services through patients' eyes, which encouraged them to engage with patients and respond to their needs.

Evidence to this review (Coulter 2012) highlighted how NHS staff are inhibited from focusing on patient-centred care (for which engagement is a prerequisite) by the perception that it is not as high a national priority as safety or financial management. Other barriers include feeling hidebound by procedures and regulation, the lack of a dedicated improvement team and defensive reactions from colleagues. These barriers are not unique to the NHS, but they are big hurdles that can only be overcome with concerted effort.

In a paper for this review Lemer and colleagues (2012) stressed that engagement is required throughout an organisation to improve productivity. Doctors lead teams, have great influence over how money is spent, and can make or break change programmes. Closer working between doctors, nurses, managers and others are key factors in engagement. There is increasing evidence that creating time for teams to reflect on how they work together can help raise care standards.

Success will not come from a single, heroic leader; successful patient-centred care programmes depend on engaged staff from ward to board being willing to try different ways of working. Key elements of patient-centred care strategies are listed in the box opposite.

Implementing a patient-centred care strategy

Luxford *et al* based their work on case studies and interviews in a range of different organisations including hospitals, doctors' practices and community organisations. They identify the following list of factors that are critical in assuring the quality of patients' experience of care:

- strong committed senior leadership

- communication of strategic vision

- engagement of patients and families

- sustained focus on employee satisfaction

- regular measurement and feedback reporting

- adequate resourcing for care delivery design

- building staff capacity to support patient-centred care

- accountability and incentives

- culture strongly supportive of change and learning (Luxford *et al* 2011).

Engaging doctors

It is a striking feature of the NHS that it employs some of the brightest people in the country, then disempowers and alienates many of them. Consultants are more likely to say they work 'at' rather than 'for' a trust, and doctors often underestimate both their power and responsibility when it comes to improving quality and productivity.

But being a doctor often doesn't feel powerful. They may have no budget, no status to make demands on the administration, no power to hire and fire, and little influence over the organisation's goals. Yet the decisions they take not only have a profound impact on patients, but on the quality of care, productivity and reputation of their employer.

Many doctors and much of the medical establishment have been in open rebellion against the government over the latest reforms. Managers and doctors need to work together to turn that opposition into engagement in making the new system work for patients. Strengthening medical engagement means ditching any notion of doctors following where managers lead in favour of managers and clinicians sharing power on the basis of mutual professional respect, united around the goal of improving quality. For some this will require a profound change in their mindset.

There is a growing literature around medical effectiveness which debunks the idea that doctors can simply keep their head down and concentrate on clinical work. In the age of increasing specialisation and multidisciplinary working, being a medical expert is no longer enough to be a top doctor; you need the skills to help build, and to be a part of, an effective team. In the United Kingdom and the United States, most efforts to develop medical leadership have fallen into the trap of simply integrating doctors into management, with limited impact. Now a growing number of organisations are engaging doctors by uniting clinicians and managers around improvement.

This is illustrated by organisations such as Intermountain Healthcare in the United States (Baker 2011) and University College London Hospital NHS Foundation Trust (Bohmer 2012, p 25), both of which have a managerial culture where medical leaders are consulted and supported, while having explicit expectations of their performance. Intermountain makes clear that doctors can override procedures or targets when it is in the best interests of the patient. In other words it does not allow corporate dogma to stop the doctor doing the right thing for the patient – professional judgement wins. Top leaders genuinely devolve power and authority in these organisations in the knowledge that this is critical in delivering performance improvements.

Doctors leading improvement need different skills depending on their specialism. In a paper for this review, Richard Bohmer (2012) identifies three models of care that potentially require different leadership approaches.

- Where the diagnosis is clear and care is standardised – such as for a heart attack – leaders need to design a system to deliver the best care, then manage it to minimise variation.

- Where there are several possible diagnoses or treatments, such as for many cancers, medical leaders need to focus the team on working with the patient to select the best options. The leader must understand how the team works and what will help it perform best.

- Where the diagnosis or treatment are obscure, such as with some rare diseases, clinicians must search for an explanation and craft a solution for each patient. The leader needs to foster experimentation leading to diagnosis and treatment, while helping the team cope with uncertainty and failure. In effect, they must lead learning.

The co-existence of different models for delivering care in one organisation has several implications for senior leaders, argues Richard Bohmer (2012). A nuanced approach that is sensitive to these differences in care is better achieved by medical leaders working at the front line with patients than by senior leaders in the organisation's corporate offices. So the authority to reconfigure clinical systems, as well as accountability for these systems' performance, must be distributed down the organisation to the frontline medical leaders.

Empowered frontline medical leaders need several resources to do their work. Most importantly they need unwavering support from senior leaders who can protect their time and provide mentoring and access to ongoing education. They need senior leaders to provide clear performance expectations and also a strong sense of the organisation's values to guide their decision-making as they make changes to improve care systems. And most importantly, since they are the ones who must reconcile the needs of individual patients with the needs of populations, they need up-to-date process, outcome and patient experience data.

The medical engagement scale

The NHS Institute for Innovation and Improvement and the Academy of Medical Royal Colleges, in conjunction with Applied Research Ltd, developed a medical engagement scale based on the idea that organisational systems play a key role in determining whether a doctor is likely to become engaged. The Index of Medical Engagement has three aspects: working in an open culture; having purpose and direction; and feeling valued and empowered. Data from almost 30 hospitals revealed a strong association between medical engagement and performance measured by the Care Quality Commission (Spurgeon *et al* 2011).

A related study by the NHS Institute and the Academy highlighted by Clark (2012) for this review identified the lessons from seven NHS organisations with the highest levels of medical engagement. All acknowledged it took time and was often challenging, and disengagement could be sudden and precipitous. But they highlighted consistent benefits such as successful initiatives, innovation, staff satisfaction and retention, improved organisational performance and better patient outcomes. The organisations emphasised that engagement should be persistent and reach the entire medical workforce, not just those at the top.

Further evidence for the benefits of medical engagement is provided in the study undertaken by McKinsey and the Centre for Economic Performance at the London School of Economics (Dorgan *et al* 2010). Their work examined the performance of around 1,300 hospitals across Europe and the United States. Overall they found that hospitals that are well managed produce higher quality patient care and improved productivity, including significantly lower mortality rates and better financial performance. Importantly, those organisations with clinically qualified managers produced better results and gave managers higher levels of autonomy.

Noting the wide variation in management scores, the United Kingdom was found to have comparatively strong management practices relative to its health care expenditure. However, the UK sample had the lowest proportion of managers with a clinical degree out of the seven countries studied. This further reinforces the need for a continued focus on clinical engagement.

One approach to giving doctors more control is service line management, developed by McKinsey and regulator Monitor to devolve decision-making and accountability to clinicians. It assumes clinical departments can be run much like commercial business units, with clinicians having considerable autonomy in allocating resources, shaping the service and setting goals.

A 2012 study of service line management for The King's Fund (Foot *et al* 2012) concluded that realising the benefits requires skilful implementation. The roles of the board and executive management need to be rethought to enable decision-making to be devolved, and clinician engagement is essential – service line management alone is not enough to engage key staff. For service line management to work, doctors need development and support, such as training in managing staff and budgets, business planning and organisational change.

These findings echo Richard Bohmer's (2012) evidence to this review.

Experience from the United States

The Institute for Healthcare Improvement in the United States has developed a framework for how organisations can improve medical engagement. This includes:

- discovering common purpose, such as improving outcomes and efficiency

- reframing values to make doctors partners in, not customers of, the organisation, and promoting individual responsibility for quality

- fine-tuning engagement to reach different types of staff – identifying and encouraging champions, educating leaders, developing project management skills and working with laggards

- using improvement methods such as performance data in a way which encourages buy-in rather than resistance

- making it easy for doctors to do the right thing for patients

- supporting clinical leaders all the way to the board

- involving doctors from the beginning – working with leaders and early adopters, choosing messages and messengers carefully, making doctor involvement visible, communicating candidly and often, and valuing doctors' time by giving management time to them.

The experience at McLeod Regional Medical Center (*see* box, below) highlights the essential features of medical engagement, especially the practice of doctors engaging with each other to drive learning, quality and professional satisfaction. There is an important message here – the key thing is not to get doctors to engage with the organisation *per se*, so much as engage with their peers in improving quality.

McLeod Regional Medical Center, South Carolina

The study by Gosfield and Reinertsen (2010) of how McLeod Regional Medical Center in South Carolina used medical engagement to secure major quality advances highlights how visitors 'marvel at the enthusiastic, effective leadership and participation of McLeod's doctors in quality, safety and value initiatives – without any significant financial incentives'. McLeod's techniques for engaging doctors include:

- asking doctors to lead improvement – the mantra is 'physician-led, data-driven, evidence-based'

- asking doctors what they want to work on – McLeod initiates about 12 major improvement efforts each year, based on doctors' recommendations

- making it easy for doctors to lead and participate – McLeod provides good support staff for improvement and does not waste doctors' time

- recognising doctors who lead, including the opportunity to present to the board

- supporting medical leaders when obstructed by difficult colleagues

- providing development opportunities – McLeod helps doctors learn about quality, safety and human factors.

Engaging future medical leaders

Junior doctors are a large but undervalued part of the medical workforce. Their 'junior' status means too little effort is made to engage them in improvement or to develop their leadership skills. For example, they regularly undertake audits as part of their training, but this valuable intelligence about service performance is little used in quality and productivity work.

The importance of identifying and nurturing future medical leaders is gradually being recognised at national, deanery and local levels. The Medical Leadership Competency Framework (now part of the new NHS Leadership Framework) developed by the NHS Institute and the Academy of Medical Royal Colleges requires all doctors to develop leadership skills, and a number of trusts and deaneries are integrating leadership and service improvement into training programmes for junior doctors.

Indeed, models of distributed medical leadership – the counter to heroic leadership – depend on the presence of leadership skills throughout delivery organisations, not only at the top. Encouraging junior doctors to practise medical leadership – such as by articulating a vision and goals, clarifying the mechanism of attaining them, and demonstrating openness and transparency – helps create a generation of engaged medical leaders.

There are also several programmes where engagement between doctors and managers is promoted through junior doctors and management trainees or other managers undertaking leadership development together. For example, the London Deanery's Paired Learning Scheme links senior registrars with managers in their trust so they can share experiences and expertise in improving services. The idea came from Dr Bob Klaber, who during his paediatrics training was struck by how little junior doctors and managers spoke or understood each other's roles (Imperial College Healthcare NHS Trust 2012).

Junior doctors on leadership programmes interviewed by The King's Fund demonstrated extraordinary determination to make a difference. They saw their programme as a chance to escape the junior doctors' lot of back-to-back clinics and ward rounds and secure time for professional and personal development. A paper for this review by Pippa Bagnall (2012) found many participants in these programmes had positive experience but some also reported frustration on the part of some participants, especially where consultants and managers were unsupportive of junior doctors undertaking activities beyond clinical practice and unwilling to let them contribute to improvement.

These junior doctors demonstrate the potential to improve services that their leadership development unleashes, but also expose how existing structures and attitudes too often turn determination into disillusion. Junior doctors are willing to make a significant contribution beyond routine clinical care. Their capacity to lead must be acknowledged and embraced much earlier in their education and training, and leadership development should be part of every medical curriculum. Their leadership skills need to be given the same standing as research and academic excellence, because the impact will be at least as great.

Engaging junior doctors in improving services: A School of Clinical Leadership

The Kent, Surrey and Sussex Postgraduate Deanery set up a School of Clinical Leadership in 2009 to teach junior doctors clinical leadership through improving services. The training changes the way many participants view their role, and they continue their engagement in improving services back at work. A typical comment was: 'With no formal training in leadership or management, I had never seen either of these things as a formal part of my role as a clinician, but I now understand how important it is to be involved. From our daily experiences of clinical care we are in a perfect position to identify needs and possibilities for positive changes.'

NHS London's development of emerging medical leaders

In 2009 NHS London and the London Deanery introduced clinical leadership fellowships (then known as Darzi fellowships) to produce high-performing clinicians to lead improvement. Fellows participate in a leadership programme and are mentored by their medical director for a year while leading change projects.

Participants rated the experience as very good or excellent. Comments included 'a privilege' and 'life-changing' (Bagnall 2012, p 10). The vast majority said they would now approach work differently, through increased self-awareness, better understanding of the contribution of others, better analytical skills, the ability to use management techniques and improved strategic thinking.

Engaging nurses and allied health professionals

Research into the role of nurse leadership in improving care (Murphy *et al* 2009) found nurse leaders encourage clinical excellence, safety and productivity. Working in a multidisciplinary team was a key ability, while participation in clinical decision-making, extending their skills throughout their career and having good support were critical factors in their development. According to Curtis and O'Connell (2011), nurses are motivated by opportunities to plan care, solve problems, make decisions and conduct research. They should be full partners in designing care pathways.

The Commission on Dignity in Care for Older People (2012) said that wards are the hubs of the multidisciplinary teams of nurses, care assistants, doctors, allied health professionals, support staff and managers responsible for care. This, the commission argued, places a particular responsibility on ward sisters and charge nurses in co-ordinating services to provide the most dignified and seamless care for each patient. They should know they have authority over care standards, dignity and wellbeing on their ward, expect to be held accountable for it, and take the action they deem necessary in the interests of patients.

In a similar vein The King's Fund summit on the care of frail older people (Cornwell 2012) concluded that team leaders in hospital wards and the community should have a higher status in their organisations, with enhanced opportunities for personal development and remuneration that reflects the value, complexity and importance of the role. This enhanced role should extend to playing a major part in recruiting their own team, controlling resources such as equipment and setting the quality of food. All care staff, especially team leaders, should see it as their responsibility to speak up if rules and working practices are undermining care.

Summit participants saw this as an important step in building an ethos of high-quality care and a supportive working environment on each ward, which would remedy many of the problems associated with poor and neglectful care of older people. Team leaders should be as closely involved with all aspects of patients' care as possible, celebrate good care and tackle poor attitudes and behaviour. The summit stressed the importance of team leaders supporting staff to engage with patients and their families to understand care from the patient's point of view.

The findings of The King's Fund summit were informed by recent research into the relationship between staff wellbeing and patients' experience of their care. This research concluded that staff wellbeing is an important factor in patient experience, and that wellbeing is affected by employee experiences at work and by individual skills and work orientations. High levels of job control helped to cushion the negative effects of high job demands and exhaustion on wellbeing. Also important is the climate of care with climates emphasising patient care being especially influential. Team leaders had a key role in setting expectations of values, behaviours and attitudes to support the delivery of patient-centred care (Maben *et al* 2012).

Engaging nurses and therapists in improving care for people

Guy's and St Thomas' NHS Foundation Trust realised the skills needed to improve the care of older people, such as communication, empathy and teamworking, were rarely developed for the nurses carrying out the work (Jensen undated). Senior nurses, ward sisters and charge nurses, doctors and therapists planned a cultural change programme for all nursing staff in the elderly care unit, alongside therapists and other clinicians.

The shutting and refurbishing of each ward gave staff a rare opportunity to train as a team. The programme focused on patient experience by using simulation techniques including actors and high-tech manikins. Staff developed a greater sense of responsibility for their own behaviour and that of colleagues, and learned to communicate more effectively with each other and the patients. By the end they were more skilled in empathising with patients' needs and feelings and helping them and their families make informed choices. The biggest benefit was engaging clinical staff in developing their own solutions to care issues.

Engaging boards

One of the consequences of the failures exposed at Bristol Royal Infirmary and Mid Staffordshire NHS Foundation Trust has been the Department of Health's drive to improve the governance and leadership performance of boards.

In 2009 the Healthcare Commission outlined three roles for boards: formulating strategy, ensuring accountability and shaping culture (Healthcare Commission 2009). There has been little research on the impact of boards on organisational performance, but two studies (Emslie 2007; Storey *et al* 2010) indicate that organisations whose boards focus on strategy and governance perform better, while boards that engage staff in decision-making raise staff satisfaction.

For anyone still clinging to the heroic model of leadership there was also evidence that excessively assertive chief executives – which can be taken as a euphemism for bullying – seriously undermine board performance. Chambers and colleagues (2011) found that high-performing trusts were more likely to have a chief executive who had been in post for at least four years, have a higher proportion of women on the board and have non-executive directors who make a significant contribution to meetings.

The ultimate test of any board is the trust's culture. In evidence for this review Alimo-Metcalfe (2012) said that putting quality at the heart of all the trust does requires:

- board members to model the appropriate engaging leadership behaviours in the way they work together and in every other relationship – from patients and families to staff and external partners

- the board to communicate to all staff the importance of adopting an engaging style of leadership that encourages innovation

- the board to understand how the culture of the organisation feels to staff, patients, their families and others, taking action where needed. Boards cannot know instinctively if staff and patients feel engaged; surveys and other measures should track organisational culture.

Given the evidence reported earlier (pp 4–6), boards should pay close attention to the results of the NHS staff survey, especially those relating to whether staff would recommend their organisation as a place to work and be treated.

Boards and staff wellbeing

As well as focusing on the health of patients, it is important boards consider the health and wellbeing of their staff. Stress harms care. In 2009 the Boorman Review of the mental health of NHS staff (Department of Health 2009a) found a strong link between stress and poor trust performance. Of the staff interviewed for the study, 80 per cent admitted their levels of anxiety, stress and depression influenced the quality of their care.

The Royal College of Nursing told this review that a survey of its safety representatives found stress was the biggest safety issue for nurses. One explanation for the impact of stress on performance is a study by Svenson and Maule (1993) which showed how it reduces higher-order thinking, including problem-solving, creativity and decision-making.

In one of the lectures undertaken as part of this review, Elisabeth Buggins, chair of Birmingham Women's NHS Foundation Trust, argued that poor care was rooted in failing to provide emotional support for staff while constantly demanding that they expend emotional energy in providing care. This, she believes, undermines their sense of vocation and blunts their understanding of the consequences of poor care.

Boards that care about staff wellbeing will, Buggins suggests, treat staff with the same respect accorded to patients, consider and manage the impact on staff when taking tough decisions, and address poor leadership and behaviour quickly. Non-executive directors will spend time getting to know what it feels like to work there, engagement levels will be monitored and published, and staff at all levels who exemplify the values of engaged leadership will be recognised and celebrated.

Since boards need a culture of innovation in their organisation, they must create 'readiness for change'. This is the extent to which staff accept the need for change, and believe it will benefit themselves and the organisation. It is a significant indicator of the chances of successfully implementing a change strategy. A Canadian hospital study by Cunningham and colleagues (2002) found readiness for change was increased when staff felt their jobs were challenging, they had considerable autonomy and they had the support and encouragement to feel confident they could cope with it.

Engaging across the system

The complexity of the government's health reforms pushes to the fore the issue of leading and engaging not just within organisations, but across systems. Failures in care quality often stem from poor co-ordination between services, and many of the efficiencies needed to deliver Quality, Innovation, Productivity and Prevention (QIPP) rely on redesigning pathways across providers, agencies and sectors. Much of the narrative has been about taking power from 'bureaucrats' and putting it in the hands of clinicians, but this is an inadequate description of leadership for such profound changes.

One certainty amid this confusion is that success in driving both quality and efficiency demands new levels of co-operation and partnership-working across systems, notably between hospital and community services and between health and social care. In a report for the National School of Government John Benington and Jean Hartley (2009) stressed the importance of public service leaders focusing on systems rather than individual organisations. They called for government to champion public sector leadership development built on 'adaptive leadership' to tackle tough, complex, cross-cutting problems. Three years later, with the demands of the health reforms and the need to integrate hospital, community and social care, adopting this system approach to leadership development is now urgent.

Leadership across systems requires an ability to understand and work with different goals, cultures and business priorities from those of your own organisation. Historically dysfunctional relationships will often need to be acknowledged and worked through to create a collaborative, whole system approach for the future.

Matching leadership skills to the health reforms

In one of the lectures given as part of this review, Ciarán Devane, chief executive of Macmillan Cancer Support, highlighted the profound change in management approach the health reforms require. Instead of working in a hierarchy-driven system where power comes from authority, managers will need to exert influence, or soft power, across a matrix of organisations where decision-making structures are not defined. 'In the new world we are going into you need a wider spectrum of leadership styles than the one which is currently dominant,' he said.

Heroic leadership will not work, while engagement will be critical. Managers will need to win people round emotionally with a compelling vision, and employ political skills to get the right people in the right places to come round to their way of thinking, building communities of influence.

All this will be happening in a system where who decides what and how is unclear. The distribution of power between, for example, the health and wellbeing board, clinical commissioning group, local outpost of the NHS Commissioning Board and clinical senate is not defined. If ground rules are not agreed about how decisions will be made, Darwinian struggles for control may ensue, with different winners in different parts of the country. As Devane put it: 'That's not matrix management, that's having a fight'.

This lack of clarity is not just a local issue; the legislation fails to spell out how Monitor, the Care Quality Commission and the NHS Commissioning Board will work together, opening the way to confused leadership at the top of the care system. How they do work together may well set the tone for the rest of the NHS.

Leadership qualities for engaging across systems

Leaders who perform well in systems tend to be highly visible and thrive on collaboration and network building, which in turn encourages distributed leadership. In evidence for this review, David Welbourn and colleagues (2012) of the Cass Business School advised leaders hoping to influence systems to:

■ go out of their way to make new connections

■ have an open, enquiring mind, unconstrained by current horizons

■ embrace uncertainty and be positive about change

■ draw on as many perspectives as possible

■ ensure leadership and decision-making are distributed throughout the system

■ promote the importance of values – invest as much energy in relationships and behaviours as in delivery.

Managers involved in delivering programmes in complex systems have long focused on the importance of boundary-spanners – a term that graphically illustrates the role of sitting astride traditional silos, making connections, building engagement and resolving crises. A study of the role of 'bridge' leaders by McMullen and Adobor (2011) found they compensated for their lack of positional power by influencing, and generated goodwill among key players to secure buy-in. The Health Foundation submission to this review stressed that considerable energy could be released when leaders were able to span existing structures.

A seminar at The King's Fund on leading across the health and social care system identified a wide range of behaviours that support engaging, collaborative, cross-system working, including leaders:

■ developing and communicating a shared vision reflecting shared values. For example, work in Torbay on integrating health and social care was built around the needs of a fictional local resident

■ being emotionally intelligent and having effective negotiating, influencing and conflict resolution skills

■ understanding systems theory, and how the system itself works

■ developing middle managers.

Too often the talk around integration focuses on money and systems, with too little appreciation that integration ultimately depends on people and culture. There is no top-down, imposed way to integrate care; it will be done through distributed, engaged leadership or it will not be done at all.

But while developing leaders is critical, there was consensus at the seminar that the wider environment, system incentives and rewards were also key. As one participant said: 'No one is going to turn into a selfless leader unless we create the conditions that make working across boundaries a natural act.' The right approach is focusing on outcomes, such as by emphasising accountability for a population (which should be the natural focus of health and wellbeing boards), rather than a service, developing a payment system that encourages integration, and holding people to account for patient experience and outcomes across the care pathway, not just within their institution.

Total Place is an initiative that looks at how a 'whole area' approach can lead to better public services at less cost. It was piloted in 13 sites under the previous Labour government with some successes, including closer co-operation between social care and the NHS. Total Place has now morphed into the Community Budgets initiative to develop an integrated approach for troubled families. These projects are worthwhile but they risk papering over the cracks of a disjointed system rather than identifying the financial, structural and cultural problems that are creating the silos of funding and thinking.

The role of GPs in system engagement

With the advent of clinical commissioning groups GPs are central to system reform. GPs have always worked across systems, but they are now expected to lead and shape them. The cultural leap they will have to make is huge.

Many doctors go into general practice because they thrive on the close relationship with patients and value independence. Some have now been thrust to the centre of a complicated, poorly defined and constantly changing network where they will have to sacrifice patient time to work on system management and service improvement. For GP leaders, engagement is now a core skill.

In recent guidance the Royal College of General Practitioners (2012) spelt out what this means: 'Patients and staff will look to GPs to influence and help determine the future direction of services; in leading and managing change there is a need for you... to understand yourself, how you can work effectively with your teams and others, and how to take people with you.' Among the people they will have to take with them are other GPs.

If clinical commissioning groups are to feel and work differently from primary care trusts they need to engage all the GPs in the area, to secure the best data, insights and ideas to reshape care pathways. This means making a reality of the idea that clinical commissioning groups should be membership organisations made up of constituent practices who share responsibility for the work of groups and their performance. Effective GP leaders will be those who are able to engage other GPs in the work of clinical commissioning groups to deliver improvements in population health outcomes and patient care.

To make this point is to reiterate one of the key messages from The King's Fund's 2011 leadership review, namely the importance of followership as well as leadership. Put simply, leadership is a relationship between leaders and followers rather than a property of individuals and teams. Making the case for effective leadership and its development therefore necessarily entails also making the case for followership and its development to avoid leaders being set up to fail. This in turn suggests that leadership development needs to be complemented by an investment in organisation development throughout the NHS, but especially in clinical commissioning groups at this stage in their formation.

Engaging across the health and social care system to integrate services

Southern Health NHS Foundation Trust is a newly merged organisation providing community and mental health services across Hampshire. Leaders of the organisation knew that its strategy of providing integrated care meant staff working for the trust and other provider organisations needed to behave differently. Key to making this happen was working with their partners to identify the leadership roles most critical to driving change throughout the health and social care system, then bringing these diverse groups together to develop their leadership capability and build relationships and trust.

Systems were put in place to reward individuals and teams whose behaviour supported the objective of integration. This work has helped secure significant reductions in hospital admissions and length of stay for frail older people, reduced dependency on inpatient care in mental health and delivered a joint response with social care to the needs of patients.

Conclusions

This review picks up where The King's Fund's Commission on Leadership and Management in 2011 finished. It shows how replacing the heroic model of leadership with one that seeks to distribute influence and decision-making throughout the organisation is essential if the NHS is to rise to the challenges that it faces. Successful leaders will be those who engage staff, patients and partner organisations in improving patient care and population health outcomes.

The business case for leadership and engagement is compelling. As we have shown, organisations with engaged staff deliver a better patient experience and have fewer errors and lower infection and mortality rates. Financial management is stronger, staff morale and motivation are higher and there is less absenteeism and stress.

This report has emphasised staff engagement because of evidence that engaged staff deliver better outcomes for patients. Equally important is the need to do much more to engage patients themselves both collectively and individually. The benefits of patient engagement include the delivery of more appropriate care and improved outcomes, especially for patients with long-term conditions.

Making a reality of leadership and engagement for improvement requires actions at all levels, from the NHS Commissioning Board to the teams delivering care to patients. For top leaders there is a need to balance a pace-setting style with a more nuanced approach in which leaders give greater priority to patient and staff engagement, especially the involvement of doctors, nurses and other clinicians. Leadership across systems is significantly under-developed in the NHS and must become a higher priority.

To deliver its objectives every NHS organisation needs to value and support leadership and engagement, for example through effective appraisals, clear job design and a well-structured team environment. NHS boards should demonstrate through their actions that they value staff and pay attention to staff health and wellbeing. The staff engagement toolkit produced by NHS Employers offers valuable advice on what boards can do to foster engagement in their organisations.

Leadership needs to be developed in ways that break down rather than reinforce silos, with managers and clinicians training and working together. Renewed efforts must be made to engage doctors and other clinicians in leadership roles, given the evidence presented in this report on the relationship between medical engagement and organisational performance. The unifying vision for every leader should be engaging for improvement with a clear focus on improving patient care and population health outcomes.

The NHS Leadership Academy is well placed to build on recent progress in leadership development and to work with NHS organisations to develop leadership and engagement. The Academy should work with leadership experts across the public and private sectors in taking on its responsibilities. This includes supporting fledgling organisations such as clinical commissioning groups as they start to get to grips with their role.

The Academy also has an opportunity to give greater priority to emerging and future leaders, alongside the support provided to top leaders. The NHS has a good track record of supporting future leaders through the graduate management training scheme and work with junior doctors, and it is important that this is taken forward in the next phase of reform. Cutting funding for training and development is an easy target when budgets are under pressure but the temptation to do so should be resisted if there is a serious commitment to build a cadre of leaders able to navigate the treacherous waters that lie ahead.

Appendix: Submissions to the review

The review sought evidence from individuals and organisations. They were invited to submit their views on leadership for engagement and submit examples of good practice. We are grateful to the following organisations who submitted evidence to the review.

- Advancing Quality Alliance (AQuA)
- Diagnosis
- Faculty of Medical Leadership and Management
- The Health Foundation
- Kent Surrey and Sussex Deanery
- NHS Employers
- NHS London
- The Patients Association
- Royal College of Anaesthetists
- Royal College of GPs
- Royal College of Nursing
- Royal College of Physicians
- Royal College of Psychiatrists
- Royal College of Surgeons
- Sandwell and West Birmingham Hospitals NHS Trust
- Sheffield Hallam University
- University College London Hospitals NHS Foundation Trust

To support the review we also commissioned a number of expert papers on different aspects of leadership and engagement for improvement.

Alimo-Metcalfe B (2012). *Engaging Boards: The relationship between governance and leadership, and improving the quality and safety of patient care.*

Bagnall P (2011). *Facilitators and Barriers to Leadership and Quality Improvement.*

Bohmer R (2012). *The Instrumental Value of Medical Leadership.*

Clark J (2012). *Medical Engagement: Too important to be left to chance.*

Coulter A (2012). *Leadership for Patient Engagement.*

Lemer C, Allwood D, Foley T (2012). *Improving NHS Productivity: The secondary care doctor's perspective.*

Welbourn D, Warwick R, Carnall C, Fathers D (2012). *Leadership of Whole Systems.*

West M, Dawson J (2012). *Employee Engagement and NHS Performance.*

All these papers are available at: www.kingsfund.org/leadershipreview.

References

Alimo-Metcalfe B (2012). *Engaging Boards: The relationship between governance and leadership and improving the quality and safety of patient care* [online]. Available at: www.kingsfund.org.uk/leadershipreview (accessed on 18 April 2012).

Alimo-Metcalfe B, Alban-Metcalfe J (2008). *Engaging Leadership: Creating organisations that maximise the potential of their people.* London: Chartered Institute of Personnel and Development.

Bagnall P (2011). *Facilitators and Barriers to Leadership and Quality Improvement* [online]. Available at: www.kingsfund.org.uk/leadershipreview (accessed on 5 March 2012).

Baker G (2011). *The Roles of Leaders In High-Performing Health Care Systems.* London: The King's Fund. Available at: www.kingsfund.org.uk/publications/articles/leadership_papers/the_roles_of_leaders.html (accessed on 5 March 2012).

Benington J, Hartley J (2009). *Whole Systems Go!: Improving leadership across the whole public service system.* Ascot: National School of Government. Available at: www.systemicleadershipinstitute.org/wp-content/uploads/2011/05/wholesystemsgopaper.pdf (accessed on 17 April 2012).

Bohmer R (2012). *The Instrumental Value of Medical Leadership: Engaging doctors in improving services* [online]. Available at: www.kingsfund.org.uk/leadershipreview (accessed on 18 April 2012).

Chambers N, Pryce A, Li Y, Poljsak P (2011). *Spot the Difference: A study of boards of high performing organisations in the NHS.* Manchester: Manchester Business School.

Clark J (2012). *Medical Engagement: Too important to be left to chance* [online]. Available at: www.kingsfund.org.uk/leadershipreview (accessed on 18 April 2012).

Commission on Dignity in Care for Older People (2012). *Delivering Dignity: Securing dignity in care for older people in hospitals and care homes. A report for consultation.* London: Local Government Association/NHS Confederation/Age UK. Available at: www.nhsconfed.org/Documents/dignity.pdf (accessed on 17 April 2012).

Cornwell J (2012). *The Care of Frail Older People with Complex Needs: Time for a revolution.* London: The King's Fund.

Coulter A (2012). *Leadership for Patient Engagement* [online]. Available at: www. kingsfund.org.uk/leadershipreview (accessed on 18 April 2012).

Cunningham CE, Woodward CA, Shannon HS, MacIntosh J, Lendrum B, Rosenbloom D, Brown J (2002). 'Readiness for organizational change: A longitudinal study of workplace, psychological and behavioral correlates'. *Journal of Occupational and Organizational Psychology*, vol 75, pp 377–92.

Curtis E, O'Connell R (2011). 'Essential leadership skills for motivating and developing staff'. *Nursing Management*, vol 18, no 5, pp 32–5.

Department of Health (2011a). *Developing the NHS Commissioning Board* [online]. Available at: www.dh.gov.uk/en/Publicationsandstatistics/Publications/ PublicationsPolicyAndGuidance/DH_128118 (accessed on 18 April 2012).

Department of Health (2011b). *NHS Staff Survey*. London: Department of Health. Available at: www.nhsstaffsurveys.com/cms (accessed on 17 April 2012).

Department of Health (2010). *Equity and Excellence: Liberating the NHS*. Cm 7881. London: Department of Health. Available at: www.dh.gov.uk/en/ Publicationsandstatistics/Publications/PublicationsPolicyAndGuidance/ DH_117353 (accessed on 17 April 2012).

Department of Health (2009a). *NHS Health and Well-being Review*. London: Department of Health. Available at: www.dh.gov.uk/en/Publicationsandstatistics/ Publications/PublicationsPolicyAndGuidance/DH_108799 (accessed on 17 April 2012).

Department of Health (2009b). *The NHS Constitution for England* (2009 edition). London: Department of Health. Available at: www.dh.gov.uk/en/ Publicationsandstatistics/Publications/PublicationsPolicyAndGuidance/ DH_093419 (accessed on 17 April 2012).

Department of Health (2008). *High Quality Care for All: NHS next stage review final report*. Cm 7432. London: Department of Health. Available at: www.dh.gov. uk/en/Publicationsandstatistics/Publications/PublicationsPolicyAndGuidance/ DH_085825 (accessed on 17 April 2012).

Department of Health (2005). *Taking Healthcare to the Patient: Transforming NHS ambulance services*. London: Department of Health. Available at: www.dh.gov. uk/en/Publicationsandstatistics/Publications/PublicationsPolicyAndGuidance/ DH_4114269 (accessed on 17 April 2012).

Department of Health (2000). *The NHS Plan: A plan for investment, a plan for reform.* Cm 4818-I. London: Department of Health. Available at: www.dh.gov.uk/en/Publicationsandstatistics/Publications/PublicationsPolicyAndGuidance/DH_4002960 (accessed on 17 April 2012).

Dorgan S, Layton D, Bloom N, Homkes R, Sadun R, Van Reenen J (2010). *Management in Healthcare: Why good practice really matters.* London: McKinsey & Co and Centre for Economic Performance. Available at: http://worldmanagementsurvey.org/wp-content/images/2010/10/Management_in_Healthcare_Report_2010.pdf (accessed on 17 April 2012).

Emslie SV (2007). *Exploring the Factors that Measure the Performance of Boards of Directors of NHS Foundation Trusts and Their Association Between Board and Organisational Performance.* Unpublished MSc dissertation, Birkbeck, University of London.

Foot C, Sonola L, Maybin J, Naylor C (2012). *Service-line Management: Can it improve quality and efficiency?* London: The King's Fund. Available at: www.kingsfund.org.uk/publications/slm_paper.html (accessed on 17 April 2012).

Goodrich J, Levenson R (2012). 'Supporting hospital staff to provide compassionate care: Do Schwartz Center Rounds work in English hospitals?' *Journal of the Royal Society of Medicine,* vol 105, pp 117–22. [Online: Doi 10.1258/jrsm.2011.110183]

Gosfield A, Reinertsen J (2010). *Achieving Clinical Integration with Highly Engaged Physicians* [online]. Available at: www2.providence.org/holycross/MedicalStaffServices/Documents/Interesting%20Articles/True%20Clinical%20Integration%20Gosfield%20Reinertsen%202010.pdf (accessed on 17 April 2012).

Hakanen JJ, Bakker AB, Demerouti E (2005). 'How dentists cope with their job demands and stay engaged: The moderating role of job resources'. *European Journal of Oral Sciences,* vol 113, pp 479–87.

Healthcare Commission (2009). *Safe in the Knowledge: How do NHS trust boards ensure safe care for their patients?* Available at: http://archive.cqc.org.uk/_db/_documents/Safe_in_the_knowledge_200903273451.pdf (accessed on 17 April 2012).

Imperial College Healthcare NHS Trust (2012). 'Paired learning'. Imperial College Healthcare NHS Trust website. Available at: www.imperial.nhs.uk/pairedlearning (accessed on 25 April 2012).

Jensen H (undated). 'RCN Older People Resource: Best practice gallery'. RCN website. Available at: www.rcn.org.uk/__data/assets/pdf_file/0010/439444/Guys_and_Thomas.pdf (accessed on 17 April 2012).

Laschinger HKS, Leiter MP (2006). 'The impact of nursing work environments on patient safety outcomes: The mediating role of burnout/ engagement'. *Journal of Nursing Administration*, vol 5, pp 259–67.

Lemer C, Allwood D, Foley T (2012). *Improving NHS Productivity: The secondary care doctor's perspective* [online]. Available at: www.kingsfund.org.uk/leadershipreview (accessed on 17 April 2012).

Luxford K, Safran DG, Delbanco T (2011). 'Promoting patient-centred care: a qualitative study of facilitators and barriers in healthcare organizations with a reputation for improving the patient experience'. *International Journal for Quality in Healthcare*, vol 23, no 5, pp 510–5. doi: 10.1093/intqhc/mzr024

Maben J, Peccei R, Adams M, Robert G, Richardson A, Murrells T (2012). *Patients' Experiences of Care and the Influence of Staff Motivation, Affect and Well-being*. Final report. National Institute for Health Service Delivery and Organisation programme HS&DR Project (08/1819/213). Available at: www.netscc.ac.uk/hsdr/projdetails.php?ref=08-1819-213 (accessed on 25 April 2012).

MacLeod D, Clarke N (2009). *Engaging for Success: Enhancing performance through employee engagement*. London: Department for Business, Innovation and Skills. Available at: www.bis.gov.uk/files/file52215.pdf (accessed on 17 April 2012).

Mauno S, Kinnunen U, Ruokolainen M (2007). 'Job demands and resources as antecedents of work engagement: A longitudinal study'. *Journal of Vocational Behavior*, vol 70, pp 149–71.

McMullen RS, Adobor H (2011). 'Bridge leadership: a case study of leadership in a bridging organization'. *Leadership & Organization Development Journal*, vol 32, no 7, pp 715–35.

Mid Staffordshire NHS Foundation Trust Inquiry (Chair: Robert Francis) (2011). 'Closing submissions'. Available at: www.midstaffspublicinquiry.com/node/505 (accessed on 17 April 2012).

Murphy J, Quillinan B, Carolan M (2009). 'Role of clinical nurse leadership in improving patient care'. *Nursing Management*, vol 16, no 8, pp 26–8.

NHS Employers (2012). *Engaging Your Staff: the NHS staff engagement resource* [online]. Available at: www.nhsemployers.org/SiteCollectionDocuments/Staff%20engagement%20toolkit.pdf (accessed on 11 May 2012).

NHS Leadership Academy (2012). *NHS Top Leaders Programme* [online]. Available at: www.leadershipacademy.nhs.uk/areas-of-work/national-programmes/nhs-top-leaders (accessed on 17 April 2012).

NHS National Workforce Projects (2007). *Maximising Staff Engagement: Planning for a 21st century workforce.* Manchester: NHS National Workforce Projects. Available at: www.em-online.com/download/medical_article/36269_nwp%20 max%20staff%20engag%20briefing%20v5%20in%20-%20final.pdf (accessed on 18 April 2012).

Prins JT, Hockstra-Weebers JE, Gazendam-Donofrio SM, Dillaingh GS, Bakker AB, Huisman M, Jacobs B, Heijden FM (2010). 'Burnout and engagement among resident doctors in the Netherlands: A national study'. *Medical Education*, vol 44, pp 236–47.

Royal College of General Practitioners (2012). *The GP in the Wider Professional Environment* [online]. RCGP curriculum statement 2.03, draft 3.2. Available at: www.rcgp-curriculum.org.uk/curriculum_documents/future_changes/2012_ draft_statements.aspx (accessed on 17 April 2012).

Salanova M, Agut S, Peiro JM (2005). 'Linking organizational resources and work engagement to employee performance and customer loyalty: The mediation of service climate'. *Journal of Applied Psychology*, vol 90, pp 1217–27.

Santry C (2011). 'Resilient NHS managers lack required leadership skills, DH research says'. *Health Service Journal*, 6 July. Available at: www.hsj.co.uk/news/ workforce/resilient-nhs-managers-lack-required-leadership-skills-dh-research-says/5032248.article (accessed on 18 April 2012).

Shaller D, Darby C (2009). *High-performing Patient and Family-centered Academic Medical Centers: Cross-site summary of six case studies.* Report prepared for the Picker Institute. Available at: www.upstate.edu/gch/about/special/picker_ report_7_09.pdf (accessed on 17 April 2012).

Spurgeon P, Clark J, Ham C (2011). *Medical Leadership: From the dark side to centre stage.* London: Radcliffe Publishing.

Storey J, Holti R, Winchester N, Green R, Salaman G, Bate P (2010). *The Intended and Unintended Outcomes of New Governance Arrangements Within the NHS.* Executive summary for the National Institute for Health Research Service Delivery & Organisation Programme. SDO Project (08/1618/129). Southampton: National Institute for Health Research Evaluations, Trials and Studies Co-ordinating Centre. Available at: www.netscc.ac.uk/hsdr/projdetails.php?ref=08-1618-129 (accessed on 17 April 2012).

Svenson O, Maule AJ (eds) (1993). *Time Pressure and Stress in Human Judgement and Decision-Making*. New York: Plenum Press.

The King's Fund (2011). *The Future of Leadership and Management in the NHS: No more heroes*. London: The King's Fund. Available at: www.kingsfund.org.uk/publications/nhs_leadership.html (accessed on 17 April 2012).

Volandes AE, Ferguson LA, Davis AD, Hull NC, Grenn MJ, Chang Y, Deep K, Paashe-Orlow MK (2011). 'Assessing end-of-life preferences for advanced dementia in rural patients using an educational video: a randomized controlled trial'. *Journal of Palliative Medicine*, vol 14, pp 169–77.

Welbourn D, Warwick R, Carnall C, Fathers D (2012). *Leadership of Whole Systems* [online]. Available at: www.kingsfund.org.uk/leadershipreview (accessed on 17 April 2012).

West M, Dawson J (2012). *Employee Engagement and NHS Performance* [online]. Available at: www.kingsfund.org.uk/leadershipreview (accessed on 17 April 2012).

West MA, Borrill CS, Dawson JF, Scully J, Carter M, Anelay S, Patterson MG, Waring J (2002). 'The link between the management of employees and patient mortality in acute hospitals'. *International Journal of Human Resource Management*, vol 13, pp 1299–310.

West MA, Guthrie JP, Dawson JF, Borrill CS, Carter MR (2006). 'Reducing patient mortality in hospitals: The role of human resource management'. *Journal of Organizational Behavior*, vol 27, pp 983–1002.